I LOVE

Sundays

MAKING SUNDAY THE
BEST DAY OF YOUR WEEK

Hal Seed

I Love Sundays

© 2015 by Hal Seed

All rights reserved. No part of this book may be reproduced in any form or by any electronic or mechanical means, including storage and retrieval systems, photocopy, recording, scanning, or other, without permission in writing from the publisher, except by a reviewer who may quote brief passages in a review.

Published by Outreach, Inc., Colorado Springs, CO 80919

www.Outreach.com

All Scripture quotations are taken from THE HOLY BIBLE, NEW INTERNATIONAL VERSION®, NIV®. Copyright © 1973, 1978, 1984, 2011 by Biblica, Inc.® Used by permission. All rights reserved worldwide.

ISBN: 9781942027188

Cover and Interior Design by Tim Downs

Printed in the United States of America

Contents

Chapter 1

Why I Came Back to Church

When I was little, my favorite moment of the day came just after 6:00 p.m. That was when Dad got home from work. I would hear his key in the door lock and run to meet him. As I got near enough for him to reach for me, I found myself lifted seven feet off the ground. Dad would hold me over his head, then pull me close to his chest. While inhaling the strong scent of his after-shave, I'd shout, "Daddy's home!"

That's the experience everyone ought to have every time they come to church.

The Lord intends it to be that way. The Bible says, "Enter his gates with thanksgiving and his courts with praise" (Psalm 100:4). God wants Sunday to be the best day of your week and the Sunday worship service to be the best hour of your day.

God wants Sunday to be the best day of your week and the Sunday worship service to be the best hour of your day.

Unfortunately, it doesn't always work out that way. Sundays can be the best of times if you'll let them. They can also be a waste of time, depending on how you treat them. The value of every Sunday depends on the importance you place on it.

For many people, a positive Sunday experience is a hit-and-miss proposition. Some Sundays are great, others not so much. Some people find Sundays boring or painful. Others use Sundays as a "catch-up" day. For them, Sundays can be frantic. Still other people use this first day of the week as a vacation day—away from God and from work.

How can you make Sunday the best day of your week? I can't

guarantee every Sunday will be perfect, but I can promise that if you will practice the seven suggestions I'm about to give you, you will begin to love Sundays, see your church as an extended family, and look forward to being with them every weekend.

What Makes Sunday Special?

Why do some people have great church experiences while others don't?

A few years ago, Craig Morgan sang about what he loved about Sunday:

> That's what I love about Sunday:
>
> Sing along as the choir sways;
>
> Every verse of Amazin' Grace . . .[1]

Craig describes interacting with his pastor, going home to a great meal and some family time, taking a nap, and a whole bunch of other things that sound old-fashioned on the surface but really refreshing in our fast-paced society. The song has more than five million hits on YouTube, which tells me that Craig is onto something. There's a lot to love about Sundays, isn't there? Maybe moving backward a bit could help us move forward a lot.

Back in the 1950s and '60s, church attendance was as American as apple pie. It wasn't an option; it was something you *did*. Today, Sundays are full of options. Where I live, the beach, the NFL, the golf course, the Internet, and the kids' sports all compete with "church time." More and more people are choosing these alternatives to church. And more and more people are wondering why life isn't working so well for them.

Picture a graph in your mind. The vertical line represents happiness and prosperity. The horizontal line represents years on a calendar. Plot the percentage of our nation's church attendance year by year. You'll notice it's been going down for the last few decades. Then plot the percentage of societal happiness and prosperity over the same length of time. What you find are two lines that run parallel. The higher the church attendance, the higher the happiness quotient. Why is that?

There's something you can't see, touch, taste, or smell about church attendance that makes it the most powerful investment of your week. Something about being in church makes us better and qualifies us for special blessings and provisions from God. Unless you understand this, you can spend a lot of time messing around with ways to make your life better when the real solution is to start with God and His Church. That's what I want to show you in these short pages: how to make your life better by strategically deciding to invest in a weekly Sunday experience.

If you've seen the movie *Titanic*, you know that something you can't see can do more damage than you can imagine. Leonardo DiCaprio's character Jack Dawson died, along with thousands of others, because of an iceberg. If you could see church the way God sees it, you'd understand that more help exists there than you can see on the surface. Church attendance and participation can have a supernatural effect on you. So here's the first suggestion for getting the most out of your Sunday experience: *Decide to let Sunday be the best day of your week.* The key to a great Sunday isn't the preacher, the service, or the people. The key is *you.*

The key to a great Sunday isn't the preacher, the service, or the people. The key is you.

Decide to Let Sunday Be the Best Day of Your Week

Deciding to let Sunday be great means deciding to let God have first place in your life by giving Him the first part of your week. It means deciding to get in the car and go to church the first day of every week. It means letting Sunday be "the Lord's day" by uncluttering your Sunday schedule. It means letting this one day be dictated by God and rest and family. And it means adopting a church not just as a place you go to but as an extended family you belong to.

Church attendance is critical for the spiritual management of your life. And the tangible benefits of being in church are even more important. Sociologists have studied the benefits of church attendance. What they've found may surprise you. Those who attend church regularly . . .

- live seven and a half years longer than those who don't;[2]

- are 56 percent more likely to have an optimistic life outlook than those who don't;[3]

- are 27 percent less likely to be depressed;[4]

- are 35 percent less likely to get divorced;[5]

- have higher average levels of commitment to partners, higher levels of marital satisfaction, less thinking and talking about divorce, and lower levels of negative interaction;[6] and

- achieve higher grades, practice better time management, and experience a better sex life.[7]

Apparently, churchgoers are getting something non-churchgoers aren't. Church attendance has benefits that cascade into just about every area of your life.

Church attendance has benefits that cascade into just about every area of your life.

I Didn't Always Love Sundays

I didn't always look at church this way. In fact, I dropped out of church my first time around. Before that, every Sunday morning I'd get dressed up in my suit, clip-on bow tie, and black dress shoes. I sat dutifully in my pew, sang along with the songs, and at the proper time toddled off to Sunday school. I don't remember getting much out of it. But then, I didn't put much into it either. This was my childhood experience of church.

In the religious tradition I was part of, children got "confirmed" at age eleven or so. I went through confirmation class, received my first communion from the bishop, and was officially declared "an adult" in the church. My first adult decision was to drop out. At the back of the sanctuary that afternoon, I announced to my mother that since adults can make their own decisions, I had decided I wouldn't be coming back.

Fortunately for me, I had friends who cared enough about my

spiritual life to reintroduce me to church. During my junior year of high school, two of my best friends were consistent church attenders. They didn't push their religion on me. They just made it clear that I was welcome to join them anytime I wanted to. We played volleyball together most Sunday afternoons. At 5:00 p.m., religiously, they would say, "We've gotta go. Gotta shower up for church."

I thought they were nuts. Here we were, playing one of the greatest games ever invented, and they wanted to go sit in some old church building, doing whatever church people did. It confounded me for the longest time.

One night, curiosity got the better of me. "Mind if I come along?" I asked.

I remember feeling awkward. What should I wear? What will people there think of me? Should I bring something to do in case I get bored?

Much to my surprise, I liked it. People were friendly. They sang pretty well, and they sang like they meant it. I felt strange the next day when a woman called to say she was glad I had attended the night before. But she seemed nice enough, and harmless. So I went back the next Sunday night.

What I learned at that church began changing my life. It still surprises me to think that Sunday is now my favorite day, but it is. During the years I dropped out of church, I did a lot of fun things on Sundays, but none of them prepared me to be a better person on Monday. Few of them introduced me to the quality of people I met in church. And none of them helped me to know God better.

What about you? What are all your Sundays adding up to? Is it possible that you are only one good decision away from enjoying one of the greatest things there is to enjoy in life? Maybe it's time to start loving Sunday and making it the best day of your week! If you haven't already done so, decide today to become part of a local church. Choose one, and start attending regularly.

Chapter 2

What Church Was Meant to Be

Back when our church was smaller, I used to call every visitor on Sunday afternoon.[1] One afternoon I called Mike and Sheri Epps. Sheri answered the phone. "Hi, Sheri," I said. "I'm calling to say it was great to have you with us today. I hope you and Mike had a good experience this morning."

Sheri replied, "I am so discouraged about church. We have tried so many churches and haven't felt welcome or wanted, or that they had anything to offer us."

I couldn't help thinking, *She's so wounded; she's probably not going to like our church either.*

We finished our conversation. Before hanging up, I prayed that the Lord would lead them to a great church and reaffirmed that we would love to have them become part of our church family. I didn't really expect to see them the next Sunday. After all, people who have a great church experience must *decide* to have a great experience, and it didn't seem like she was letting herself decide to like anything about church.

To her credit, Sheri showed up the next Sunday. She even introduced herself to me. She put her kids in our PromiseLand program.[2] She and Mike sat in the third or fourth row. They came back a third week. And then a fourth, and a fifth. Somewhere along the line, the Eppses joined one of our small groups. They found places to volunteer. They started making acquaintances, then friends. Mike and Sheri have found a real home among us.

Several years ago a church demographer named Win Arn did a study of satisfied church members. He discovered they have six things in common. According to Arn, satisfied church members:

- Attend regularly

- Volunteer to serve somewhere

- Develop friendships

- Call it "my church"

- Give consistently

- Invite others

It's a helpful list. You can measure your level of church involvement right now by adding up how many of these you're doing. The more items you check, the more involved you are.

Sheri's Prayer Partner

A few months into her time at New Song Community Church, Sheri came up to me and said, "Pastor, I'd like you to find me a prayer partner." I smiled, gulped, and said I would.

What Sheri was asking for was someone she could meet and pray with every week. I've had several prayer partners over the years. What I know is, either your prayer partner becomes a very close friend or your time together each week is awkward. A prayer partner is a rare individual. The two of you have to be willing to pray out loud together. You have to be willing to be honest with each other. You have to make a commitment to each other.

I knew what Sheri was really asking for was a close friend. That's one of the wonders of church. After you attend for a while, you almost always make several good friends there. Sometimes God introduces you to a BFF.

All week long I prayed for Sheri's request. After church the following Sunday I sought her out. "Sheri," I said, "I don't think I can answer your request. I think only God can give you a prayer partner. I'll continue to pray with you about this. But I don't think it would work for me to assign you a partner. I think God has to bring you one." She nodded in agreement. We prayed together.

Two weeks later Sheri reported, "Hal, it happened! Last week, as I was dropping my daughter off in PromiseLand, I shook hands with the lady who was signing kids in. As our hands touched, I felt God say, *She's the one.* I asked her if she'd like to get together to pray, and she said she had been looking for a prayer partner. I am so excited about this relationship I can't stand it!"

A Happy Ending

Sheri and Karen prayed together for the next several years. They became great friends. They became dangerous for God together.

I wish I could tell you that every time someone asks me to pray for something, it happens. But I'm not a miracle worker. That is God's department. What I can tell you is that what Sheri did made Sunday the best day of her week. Mike and Sheri Epps have been a significant part of New Song for more than fifteen years now. Their kids have grown up here. Their character has been forged here. They have friends who brought them groceries when Mike lost his job. Dozens of us prayed with them when Mike had brain surgery. The Eppses have a deep relationship with God and a library of wonderful memories because (1) they decided to make Sundays great and (2) they did what it takes to make Sundays great by investing in the whole church experience. They attend regularly, volunteer, make friends, give consistently, and invite others. That's what makes Sunday special for them: it's their church.

Here's my second suggestion: *To get something great out of church, invest something great into church.*

> *To get something great out of church, invest something great into church.*

Spectators and Players

There's an old saying that goes, "To have a friend, you have to be a friend." It's similar in church. At a football game, you have spectators and players. Spectators attend games. Players prepare all week and spend lots of energy making sure their team wins. Spectators sometimes leave early because they're not really *invested* in their team. Players stay till the end no matter what the score. Who enjoys the game the most? The players, every time. Even when they lose, they learn something that helps them the next time out.

I played football in elementary school. But for most of my growing-up years I was a competitive swimmer. I was in the pool up to five hours a day. Then one day, I hung up my trunks. At age twenty-three I swam my last race, collected my final medal, and called it quits. The only swimming I intended for my future was splashing around with my children.

Things changed a few years ago. A friend invited me to swim in a local ocean competition. It was no fun at all. Halfway around the pier I had to rest on the lifeguard's surfboard. I was embarrassed, maybe even humiliated. The feeling goaded me to get back in the water. I started swimming a day or two a week. As I got in better shape, it started being fun again. Today, I look forward to swimming every day. I like swimming, and I like what swimming does for me. I feel better, and I like more of what I see in the mirror.

Athletes have a saying: *no pain, no gain*.

Church attendance is like that. God loves to see you worship Him, so He rewards even the most meager effort you make. But in a very real sense, the more you invest in your church, the more you get out of it.

You've probably met people who are raving fans of their church. No doubt they are highly invested there.

The Bible says, "Where your treasure is, there your heart will be also" (Matthew 6:21). In other words, *if you want to love something, invest in it.*

Mike and Sheri Epps invest in our church. They come regularly, volunteer consistently, and place 10 percent of their income in the offering every month. In Malachi 3:10 God says, "Bring the whole tithe into the storehouse, that there may be food in my house." When Mike was out of work, they tithed on Sheri's salary, even when things were tight. There's something about a sacrifice that makes us love the object of our sacrifice even more. As a result of the Eppses' sacrifices, they love their church. I think the principle goes like this: No pain, no gain. Little pain, little gain. Much pain, much gain.

Never underestimate the power of a sacrifice! Make Sunday the best day of your week by *investing* your time and treasure there. Do this and you'll discover what church was meant to be. You'll take the field every Sunday with your team—your new, extended family—and find so much more than you ever thought possible as you do life together! That's step two for loving Sundays.

Chapter 3

What You Really Want out of Church

Jill Mayfield sits in the second row at church every week. I don't know her well yet, but I know her story well. Jill is a marine. She's a single mom who's been deployed to Korea and Afghanistan and faces the challenges of caring for her daughter every time she's on a field operation, deployment, or any of a dozen other things that can take a marine away from their family. Jill found something significant when she started coming to church.

Marines are often on the move. Typically, they receive duty assignments in three-year increments. During those three years, they're likely to deploy once or twice to foreign lands. When not deployed, they conduct rigorous field training. While preparing to deploy, they do "work-ups," simulating deployment conditions for two or three weeks at time. On deployment, they're America's "tip of the spear" fighting force. Renowned for their air, land, and sea versatility, marines fight in smaller numbers than their air force, army, and navy counterparts. Like the other branches of the military, they face dangers others only read about. As a result, many of them experience some form of post-traumatic stress disorder.

One effect of such trauma is a high divorce rate. My marine friends tell me that currently, more than 70 percent of enlisted marines divorce during their first duty station. The rate goes above 90 percent for marine drill instructors. I have had more than a dozen drill instructors in my church. By God's grace, and with the support of the church, all of them have intact marriages.

Jill's Challenges

In Jill's words, "I was struggling as a single mother and a marine, feeling guilty watching my daughter cry over FaceTime when I couldn't be with her because I was in the field. Trying to sort out why things happened the way they had since I returned from deployment and my ex-husband's lack of involvement with our daughter. I felt like I was missing a foundation."

You've got challenges too. A hectic schedule. A strained marriage. Health concerns. Financial troubles. Career uncertainty. That's part of the reason church is so important. And part of the reason it's imperative to make the most of every Sunday of your life.

In Jill's case, she was open to church because she was "missing a foundation." She found that foundation when she entered into what you might call "church life." Everyone who comes to church has at least one thing in common: we're all looking for a better life. Part of that better life has to do with a God-ordained rhythm.

We're all looking for a better life. Part of that better life has to do with a God-ordained rhythm.

The Rhythm of Life

In the Bible, God prescribes fifty-two Sabbaths a year as part of our health regimen. That's seven and a half weeks of holy vacation! God did this because when He wired us up, He constructed us to run best on a rhythm of engagement and withdrawal.

In the exercise world there's a rhythm of "stress and release." In order to build solid muscles, we need to stress them so they'll grow and rest them so they'll recuperate. You can see this in the long-term pattern of annual seasons of the year, the short-term pattern of daily light and dark, and the intermediate pattern of workdays and weekends.

God made the Sabbath for release. It's part of our divinely designed nature. To make Sunday the best day of your week, recognize life's rhythm and dance to it.

To make Sunday the best day of your week, recognize life's rhythm.

Jill has figured out that in order to be her best at work on Monday, she needs to be in church on Sunday. She spends an hour every Sabbath morning worshipping God, listening to a biblically based sermon, and enjoying the company of others who are seeking God too. By building her schedule around Sundays, she's entered into God's rhythm and dance.

It wasn't always so. For a while she was living under her own strength, without God's help and the help of a church family. I can't say for sure that she wouldn't have gotten divorced, but I'm confident the church would have helped with her marriage. Right now, she's in the early stages of a relationship with a man named Larry. The church is helping them in the new relationship they're forming together.

In the Old Testament, King Solomon was called the wisest man who ever lived. He once wrote a song whose opening lyrics are:

> Unless the LORD builds the house,
>
>> the builders labor in vain.
>
> Unless the LORD watches over the city,
>
>> the guards stand watch in vain.
>
> In vain you rise early
>
>> and stay up late,
>
> toiling for food to eat—
>
>> for he grants sleep to those he loves.
>> (Psalm 127:1–2)

What Solomon is saying is, *if you want to get the most out of life, make sure God is in your life.* The race isn't won by the one who works the hardest, but by the one who works the smartest. Work hard, then rest. Stress, then release. Seek God on the Sabbath. What you gain with Him on Sunday will more than make up for whatever you might miss out on by not working that day.

Closed on Sundays

A few years ago a friend of mine opened a Chick-fil-A restaurant in town. Chick-fil-A is the most profitable fast-food restaurant on a store-by-store basis. Ask their CEO Dan Cathy why their franchises are so profitable, and he'll tell you, "Because we're closed on Sundays."

Chick-fil-A closes on Sundays so their employees can release and attend church. As a result of this rhythm, they net more income in six days than other fast-food restaurants do in seven. Do the math. Then reread Psalm 127:1–2. Honoring God's rhythm works!

What I Really Want out of Church

There are a lot of reasons why people go to church: we want to honor God, become better people, meet friends, raise great kids, develop great marriages, be part of something significant, be encouraged, ingest hope, and the list goes on. Dig deep enough, though, and you'll find that ultimately all of us who go to church want church to help us have a better life.

A few years ago I wrote a book called *The Bible Questions*.[1] My purpose was to answer people's questions about the Bible so they would want to read it more often. Why do I want people to read the Bible? Because I want people to be successful.

Most people tell me they don't read the Bible as often as they want to and not nearly as often as they should. When I ask them why, they usually say, "I don't have time! I have to work! I have to pay the bills! I have a family to take care of!"

There's an irony to this. God tells us that the best way to pay our bills and take care of our family is to read the Bible more often. Look at this verse: "Keep this Book of the Law always on your lips; meditate on it day and night, so that you may be careful to do everything written in it. Then you will be prosperous and successful" (Joshua 1:8). According to God, if you want to be successful, spend time in His Book.

Church is the place where we are all presented with the truth of the Bible. At some point during each service, a pastor or teacher opens the Bible and explains God's Word to us. I remember a Sunday twenty-some years ago when my associate pastor, Scott Evans, preached a message from "The Love Chapter" (1 Corinthians 13). This chapter contains a list of fifteen actions that describe what love is. After reading them to us, Scott said, "When you boil it all down, *love is work*."

That one sentence changed my marriage. No longer do I think that loving my wife well will just come naturally to me. If I'm going to love her the way God wants me to and the way she deserves,

I'm going to *work* at it.

I can think of dozens of other times that listening to God's Word preached has changed my approach to life. Hearing God's Word can change me, just like reading God's Word can change me.

I believe the success principle in Joshua 1:8 applies to church attendance the same way it applies to Bible reading. The power of hearing God's Word preached weekly anchors you to truth and elevates your attitudes, intentions, perspective, and behavior. The way to experience a better life is to recognize life's rhythm by releasing with God's people, around God's Word, every week.

The way to experience a better life is to recognize life's rhythm by releasing with God's people.

Releasing doesn't mean crashing on the couch in a semi-vegetative state. Clinical studies show that if you spend too much time with the television, it actually wears you out. The first two hours are restful, but after that, you do yourself damage. This is why watching an afternoon football game can be an excellent complement to a morning of worship—just be sure to get up during halftime to move around.

Biblical "releasing" is like cross-training. You release by switching gears. You can recharge by sitting in church during the service, by listening to God through the sermon, the prayers, the Lord's Supper, and other elements of worship. You can get filled up by enjoying God's people. But you can also recharge by engaging in a different kind of service than you normally do on weekdays. Handing out bulletins, welcoming guests, teaching small children, counseling teens, and a hundred other volunteer positions can be supernaturally refreshing when you do them for the Lord and with His power.

Get the most out of your church experience by dancing with the rhythm of the sacred. Be at church not just when it's convenient but every Sunday. Don't let work or recreation keep you from God's cadence for your life. When you go on vacation, use Sunday morning to encourage another church with your presence. That's suggestion three for having a great church experience: *Honor God's rhythm by celebrating the Sabbath.*

Chapter 4

How to Make Sunday the High Point of Your Week

I recently watched a video with a quote from former senator Joe Lieberman. He said, "Sometimes people say to me, 'In your life with all the responsibilities, how can you possibly stop on one day a week to observe the Sabbath?' Part of my answer is, 'How could I *not* stop?'"[1]

As a practicing Jew, Lieberman understands God's rhythm for life. Jews believe that celebrating the Sabbath is the high point of their week. We have much to learn from them.

A few years ago, I had the privilege of being at the Western Wall in Jerusalem as the Jews brought in the Sabbath together. It was a raucous celebration. Jewish men, dressed in their finest, were bobbing back and forth. Israeli soldiers, Uzis in hand, were singing Sabbath songs together. One little boy ran up to me with a huge smile on his face and shouted *Shabbat Shalom* ("Sabbath peace") to me like I was a long lost relative. It was one of the most festive celebrations I've ever seen.

Sabbath celebration is so sacred to these people that they put their elevators on automatic. To avoid even the possibility of working by pushing a button, Israeli elevators are programmed to stop and open on every floor from the beginning of the Sabbath to its end. This might seem extreme, but the effect is transcendent. Board an elevator in Israel on the Sabbath, and every stop will remind you that there is a God who created the world and He wants you to release and enjoy Him.

Jews celebrate the Sabbath on the seventh day to remind them that on the seventh day God rested from His labor of creation (Genesis 2:2–3). Because the resurrection of Jesus happened on a Sunday, Christians adopted the first day of the week as their Sabbath.

"Remember the Sabbath day," God says, "by keeping it holy. Six days you shall labor and do all your work, but the seventh day is a sabbath to the LORD your God. On it you shall not do any work, neither you, nor your son or daughter, nor your male or female servant, nor your animals, nor any foreigner residing in your towns" (Exodus 20:8–10).

Remembering and Observing

The Jews make their Sabbath special by preparing for it all week long. They do this by *remembering* and *observing*.

God, through Moses, gave the Ten Commandments twice. Once in the book of Exodus, once in the book of Deuteronomy. In Exodus 20:8 the fourth commandment reads, "Remember the Sabbath day." In Deuteronomy 5:12 it reads, "Observe the Sabbath day."

Remembering is looking back. On Sunday, Monday, and Tuesday, the Jews remember what went on during the Sabbath they just celebrated. Observing is looking forward. On Wednesday, Thursday, and Friday, they look forward to the coming Sabbath. This cycle of remembering and observing forms the sacred cadence of the Jewish week. The Sabbath is the high point of their week because they think about it all week long.

My son and I are *Lord of the Rings* fanatics. I read the books to him when he was in middle school. Every time one of the movies came out, we would talk about how excited we were in the days leading up to it and talk about how much we enjoyed it on the days afterward. That's what the Jews do with their Sabbaths.

What if we did the same?

Seeing each *The Lord of the Rings* movie on the day it came out was so important that Bryan and I cleared our schedules of anything that would keep us from attending. We phoned friends and invited them to see it with us. We went online and bought tickets in advance. We arrived at the theater early to make sure we got good seats. What if we put that kind of energy into our Sunday experience?

The Difference Between Normal and Special

For Jews, the Sabbath is the highlight of their week because they prepare for it as if it's the highlight of their week. They make it special by treating it special. On Friday afternoon, Jewish moms bake a special kind of bread called *challah* in preparation for the evening meal. They deck out the dinner table with the family's finest dishes. Shabbos candles are lit. Dad recites a prayer called "the Kiddush" to begin the evening. A song is sung welcoming the angels to the feast. Wine is poured and shared with everyone present.

Sociologists tell us there are normal events and elevated events. The difference is in the preparation. On a normal date night, a boy showers, combs his hair, and puts on clean clothes. For prom, he rents a tuxedo, buys flowers, and washes his car. The difference between "normal date" and "prom date" is in the preparation. The way to make Sunday the best day of your week is to prepare for it as if it's going to be the best day of your week.

How to Sabotage Your Sundays

On a normal weekend, the Smith family does something exciting Saturday night, sleeps until the last minute Sunday morning, rushes to get ready for church, and bickers all the way to the parking lot. What kind of a mood does that set for Sunday worship?

Fortunately, church parking lots seem to have developed supernatural powers. People get calmed there just as Jesus calmed the sea. A pastor once called his church's parking lot "miracle corner" because as people pulled in, sinners became saints, chaos became tranquility. I've seen it many times myself. A carload of competitors becomes a boatload of bliss. People who couldn't stand each other a minute ago now stroll arm in arm into the church building.

Anyone who has ever put on a plastic smile knows how difficult it is to concentrate on something wonderful when they're feeling something awful. One of the greatest things about church is that people regularly walk in a mess and walk out at peace. Imagine how much better off we would be if we walked into church already at peace? How high might our high point go then?

One of the greatest things about church is that people regularly walk in a mess and walk out at peace.

There Has to Be a Better Way

Rewind the Smiths' weekend for a minute. What if, instead of whooping it up on Saturday night, they changed their "whoop night" to Friday? What if Mr. and Mrs. Smith developed a plan for preparing for Sunday like Sunday was something worth preparing for?

Assuming the Smiths have young children, imagine this: It's Saturday morning and Mrs. Smith is asking each member of the family what they want to wear to church tomorrow. Armed with this information, she does laundry to make sure the chosen clothes are all ready by morning. On Saturday evening, Mr. Smith helps the family settle down before heading toward an early bedtime. What kind of difference would it make in your church experience if every member of your family woke up fully rested on Sunday morning?

If the Smiths have teens, they might not want to kill their adolescents' social life every weekend by insisting on an early Saturday night curfew. But parents and teens can work together to come up with a mutually acceptable plan for Sunday mornings. Discuss how long they'll need to shower, dress, and eat breakfast so that everybody can be ready with a little margin before jumping in the car.

If Mr. or Mrs. Smith is parenting alone, advanced planning can relieve a ton of stress. The marines have a saying, "Proper prior planning prevents poor performance." It applies to all of us.

Imagine if each Smith laid out his or her clothes before going to bed Saturday night. Imagine Papa Smith setting the breakfast table and Mama Smith putting out the cereal the night before. Imagine the Smiths having a standing agreement that if it takes fifteen minutes to get to church, they'll be in the car twenty-five minutes beforehand so they can drive calmly, walk across the parking lot leisurely, say hello to friends genuinely, and arrive in their seats with a few minutes to spare. Imagine being able to breathe a short "Lord, I'm grateful to be here today" prayer before the service starts. What kind of a difference might that make if you were a Smith?

Getting to Church in a Good Mood

At the beginning of Psalm 122, the writer David says, "I rejoiced with those who said to me, 'Let us go to the house of the LORD.'"

With that kind of excitement, I'm guessing that David had a preparation plan for getting his family to church in a good mood.

Imagine yourself sitting in church relaxed and happy. There's no to-do list in your head and no "I shouldn't have said that" guilt on your conscience. Friends are around you. You smile and say hi to them. You ask God to speak, and He does. You sing as if He's the audience and you're the performer, giving the performance of your life for your Lord.

A friend said to me, "I once told God that I hate Sundays because of all the hassles involved. He whispered back, 'I love Sundays because that's the day My children sing to Me.'" It's a great picture, isn't it? God up in heaven, enjoying your presence; you with your church, exalting your Lord.

God is a communicating God. The Bible says He *spoke* the world into existence (Genesis 1:3). It says He continues to speak, constantly, through the canopy of wonder above our heads (Psalm

19:1). Sometimes Christians question why God never speaks to them. I think that's the wrong question. It's not that God isn't speaking. It's that we're too busy to listen.

In my experience, God often speaks in church. He's spoken to me, and He's spoken to my friends. He wants to speak to you too.

Isaiah 58 says,

> If you call the Sabbath a delight
>> and the LORD's holy day honorable,
> and if you honor it by not going your own way
>> and not doing as you please or speaking idle words,
> then you will find your joy in the LORD,
>> and I will cause you to ride in triumph on the heights of the land. (verses 13–14)

Honoring God's Day

Church is much more than a Sunday experience. But the highlight is the Sunday service. Sunday is *game day* for church members. Knowing this, how will you prepare for next Sunday? What will you do to prepare yourself to hear the voice of God? Suggestion four for those who want to get the most out of their church experience is to *prepare for Sunday as if it's the highlight of your week*. Anticipate Sunday, plan for Sunday, and execute your plan as if you were about to attend something really important—because it really is the most important hour of the week for every believer.

> *Prepare for Sunday as if it's the highlight of your week.*

I recently officiated at the wedding of a couple named Chris and Sarah Evans. While planning the ceremony together, I asked them how they met. Sarah said, "During the first day of class my freshman year, all the students had to introduce themselves. When Chris introduced himself, I automatically said, 'Wow! This guy is great and cute and something special.' Class met once a week. So the next week, I dressed up a little bit for class."

She did that every week. Chris noticed. Now they're living happily ever after.

Sarah thought Chris was special, so she took special care on the days she went to class with him. Not a bad model to follow.

Chapter 5

How to Make Sunday the High Point of Your Children's Week

Over the last four chapters we've covered some solid principles for how to love Sundays:

1. Decide to let Sunday be the best day of your week.

2. Invest something great into church.

3. Honor God's rhythm by celebrating the Sabbath.

4. Prepare for Sunday as if it's the highlight of your week.

Those four verbs—*decide, invest, honor,* and *prepare*—describe life-altering actions. *Deciding* determines your direction. *Investing* determines your depth. *Honoring* determines your height. *Preparing* determines your bandwidth. Putting these into practice will not only alter the quality of your life but the quality of your children's lives as well.

Which brings us to what might be the most important step in making Sunday our best day: our children. Our children are our legacy. They're who live on after us.

Our children are our legacy.

Influencing the Future

How can you make Sunday the high point of the week for your children? Even better, how can you help make Sunday the high point of the week for your children *when they're grown up*?

I know this about you: if you have children, you want them to have a better life than you've had. You want them to be honest, kind, and successful. You want them to be respected by their peers. You want them to make a difference in their world.

The good news is, while you can't force your kids to have good character, the old adage is true: an acorn never falls far from the tree. You are in a position to significantly influence the outcome of your children's attitudes, actions, and behaviors when they grow up.

Scripture says, "Start children off on the way they should go, and even when they are old they will not turn from it" (Proverbs 22:6).

Your job isn't to finish your children's lives for them. You just need to start them off right. Proverbs 22:6 is my fifth suggestion for you: *Start your children off on the way they should go.*

Start your children off on the way they should go.

How do you do that?

Because I'm giving you seven suggestions for your church experience, let me give you seven for your children's experience as well:

1. Put God first.

Jesus said that if you will seek first God's kingdom and His way of doing things, everything else will pretty much fall into place (Matthew 6:33, my paraphrase).[1] He also said that when your children grow up, they will live a lot like they've seen you live (Luke 6:40, also my paraphrase).[2]

In other words, how you live could be the greatest influence on the trajectory and quality of your children's lives.

How you live could be the greatest influence on the trajectory and quality of your children's lives.

Putting God first means making Him the top priority. God's first commandment is "I am the LORD your God, . . . you shall have no other gods before me" (Exodus 20:2–3). It sounds counterintuitive, but the best gift you can give your children isn't to love them first— it's to love God first. If your heart is full of the kind of love you can get only from God, then the overflow of your heart will spill that kind of love onto your children.

Putting God first means spending time with Him, caring for what He cares about, using your money the way He would use it if it were His. Putting God first means honoring Him on the Sabbath and honoring Him with your words, attitudes, and ethics at work. Putting God first means honoring Him with how you treat your body—what you eat and how you exercise. I know, those are tall orders. And there is grace. You won't be perfect. But if you are trying to honor God, your children will see that and imitate it. And when you fail, they'll see that it's okay for them to be imperfect too.

2. Let your kids see your relationship with God.

One of the most famous Bible passages on raising children is Deuteronomy 6:6–9. These verses describe how to have your relationship with God rub off on your children. "Talk about [God's commandments] when you sit at home and when you walk along the road, when you lie down and when you get up," it says in verse 7.

In the generation that came before me, Christian families held what was called "family devotions" together. After dinner, the family would read a passage of Scripture together, then talk about it and pray together. That never worked well for me. The idea seemed forced and old-fashioned. (Ironically, the older I get, the more I seem to like "old-fashioned." There are lots of things to be admired about how previous generations lived their lives.) Ultimately I rejected that practice because I wanted everyone in my family to have a relationship with God that was real and personal. An orchestrated discussion didn't seem authentic enough.

Instead of walking through a daily devotional, Lori and I made a conscious effort to talk about our relationship with the Lord during dinner as often as possible. I would say, "Honey, tell us what you're reading in the Bible." Or, "What is God saying to you these days?" As our children got older, I'd ask them what they were reading or what they learned in Sunday school or their youth group. A favorite of ours is a game we still play called "High/Low." Everyone at the table takes a turn in describing their highest moment of the day and their lowest moment. Inevitably, someone's high or low involves God. By talking about God at the dinner table, I can communicate my relationship with Him in a natural way. Of course there are other ways of accomplishing the same thing; the point is to let your children see your relationship with God in a way that rubs off on them.

3. Let your kids see your spending.

The Bible says, "Bring the whole tithe into the storehouse, that there may be food in my house." This is so important to God that it's the only time He gives a command with permission to "test me in this." His promise is that when you faithfully bring your tithe to your local church, He will "throw open the floodgates of heaven and pour out so much blessing that there will not be room enough to store it" (Malachi 3:10).

With all the commercials out there pressuring us to buy, try, taste, wear, and use things, the concept of tithing can be a real challenge. Fortunately for us, Lori and I started tithing from our first paychecks after our honeymoon. We never got used to thinking of that money as "ours," which relieved a lot of temptation.

In America, there are two things we keep to ourselves: our sex life and our finances. I'm in complete support of keeping the first one to yourself, but what if, instead of guarding your financial privacy like it was Fort Knox, you shared it with your children?

What if, instead of talking about your budget after the kids go to sleep, you invited them into the conversation? I recently discovered that if I earn more than $32,000 a year, I'm part of the 1 percent of the wealthiest people on earth. (You can look up your exact ranking at www.globalrichlist.com.) How about calling a fun family meeting where you look this up together and rejoice at how much you have been blessed? You could use the occasion to talk about how and why you spend your money the way you do.

Then, when Johnny wants to know why he can't have that new toy, or why the family isn't going over the river and through the woods to grandma's house this Christmas, he'll understand. If you choose to give the whole tithe to your church, your children will know and be able to watch for God's Malachi 3:10 blessing in your lives. If you designate a portion of your income toward helping a child in a developing country, they'll see and learn from that as well.

The Bible says, "Everyone who is fully trained will be like their teacher" (Luke 6:40). When your children are old enough to start managing their own money, they'll emulate your values.

4. Let them tithe.

Until my kids went off to college, I distributed allowances every Sunday night. When I did so, I was careful to make sure the allowance could be split into three portions. I wanted my kids to learn the simple 10-10-80 formula for fiscal management that I believed (and still believe) would lead them to financial success in life.

The 10-10-80 formula goes like this: from everything you earn, bring 10 percent to God, save 10 percent for the future, and live on the rest. To make it easy for Bryan and Amy to tithe and save, I made sure their allowance could be split easily into tenths. When their allowance was one dollar, I tried to give it to them in the form of two dimes and other change. When it was five dollars, I made sure they had two sets of fifty cents. As soon as the kids received their money, they would run to the living room and put their first 10 percent in the "Jesus bank." Then they would take their second 10 percent and put it in their savings envelope.

I have to admit, the savings envelope didn't go perfectly. The purpose of "savings" is to accumulate for future big purchases or emergencies, and those "big purchases" seemed to come along frequently enough that the savings envelope rarely got very full. But the Jesus bank worked wonders. My kids are in their late twenties now, and to this day they love to tithe.

Lori and I figured it was too hard to remember to bring their change to church every week, so instead the money was entrusted to the Jesus bank weekly and then emptied and brought to church every month or so.

Anyone who knows me will tell you I've made a lot of mistakes in life. But the one thing I've done well is raised financially savvy offspring. Both of them paid off their college student loans within two years of graduating. Neither of them has ever been in debt since. Neither of them has ever paid rent. Bryan and his wife, Alyssa, bought their first home two weeks before they were married. Amy and her husband, Scott, paid cash for theirs. Both couples sponsor needy children in developing countries. Both of them give to Christian organizations over and above their tithes. Both of them feel financially free. It's God promise to those who tithe.

If you just read that paragraph and are tempted to feel bad, please don't. When you picked up this book, you were hoping to learn some things that would help you. If this is one of those things, I encourage you to think like the apostle Paul in Philippians 3:13–14: "Forgetting what is behind and straining toward what is ahead, I press on toward the goal to win the prize." What's behind you is behind you. Don't focus on it. Press on toward the future. It's never too late to get better, or help your children get better, no matter what age they are (or you are).

5. Serve at church together.

I once read a study published by the Leadership Network that attributed love for God and love for church to two things. The most important one was *serving God at church together*. According to the study, children whose parents served at church and found ways for their children to serve with them were far more likely to grow up to love God than children who didn't.

If you'll talk with a staff member at your church, chances are good they will be able to point you to a ministry both you and your children can enjoy doing together. For instance, it's likely that your church holds a work day now and then. Lots of families will turn out for tasks like sweeping, dusting, and landscaping. At our church, kids can start serving in our PromiseLand ministry when they are eight years old. An increasing number of churches are offering cross-cultural family missions trips. Which leads me to my sixth suggestion.

6. Send them on a cross-cultural missions trip.

The second item on Leadership Network's study of actions that helped kids love God was *going on missions trips*. Every spring break, our church's youth group has headed somewhere to serve people less fortunate than themselves. Usually, the group hosts a Vacation Bible School in a church in rural Mexico. In order to qualify for the trip, our students have to attend classes where they learn a few words of Spanish, practice the songs they'll be singing on location, and learn how to lead their particular session of the Vacation Bible School. This is great training, and the trip hasn't yet begun.

Once they reach the village, students discover two things that change them forever: (1) God can use them, and (2) they are far wealthier than they thought!

By leading the Vacation Bible School, students learn they are capable of doing great things for God. How valuable is that? And because of the living conditions they've experienced, when they return home, they tell mom and dad how grateful they are for all the things they've been given. This one-two combination is powerful in forming a young person's appreciation for who they are and how God can use them in the lives of others.

7. Help them find godly mentors.

Somewhere between the ages of eleven and fourteen, every child begins to be cool and have parents who are not. A gap starts to open in communication and influence. One of the geniuses of the local church is the youth group. In most churches, this group is led by some young adults who love God and love students. During the preteen and teenage years, these godly young adults become critical in students' spiritual journeys.

Youth pastors and youth leaders can do for your kids what you can't during their turbulent teens. Introducing your adolescent to a youth leader or two will not only help make Sunday the best day of their week but will likely make God a lifelong priority in their life.

My Dad Used to Say

I think it was Mark Twain who said that all children go through three phrases. When they are young they say, "My dad says . . ." As teens they say, "My dad doesn't know anything." And as adults they say, "My dad used to say." We'll never be perfect parents, but fortunately we don't have to be. Your children know you love them. Someday, in spite of all the things you wish you could go back and do over, they're going to quote you as one of the greatest sources of inspiration in the world. Parenting is a winning proposition! So start your children off on the way they should go.

Chapter 6

Why Churches Aren't Perfect

There's a saying among pastors that goes, "Ministry would be easy if it weren't for the people."

If you're reading this anytime close to Thanksgiving, you're probably well aware that every family has its _____ (fill in the blank: *rude, awkward, difficult*) person. You know who I'm talking about. It's your Aunt Mabel, or Uncle Harry. The person who has bad breath, makes noises, talks too much, or for any number of other reasons, is uncomfortable to be around. In my experience, every family has an Aunt Mabel or Uncle Harry at their table. If you can't figure out who that person is, it just might be you!

One of the biggest reasons people leave a church, and one of the easiest reasons people choose not to join a church, is because of people. It's also one of the worst reasons to walk away. I want to tell you why.

When God thought up the whole idea of a community of faith, He pictured a microcosm of society. He saw His Church filled with all kinds of people. We sometimes sing, "Red, brown, yellow, black, and white, they are precious in His sight. Jesus loves the little children of the world." But it's not just colors Jesus loves. He loves all shapes and sizes. He loves educated and uneducated. Wealthy and poor. Loud and soft. Kind and rude. Love-filled and hate-filled. Whole and broken.

When God designed His community, He wanted all people to be part of it. He never wanted a museum where only the beautiful and refined people would hang out. He wanted a hospital, where every disease could be healed.

God has a purpose for every type of person in His Church family. Sweet people add sweetness to the church. Salty people add salt. Salt is a preservative that makes things last longer by warding off decay. Salty people have an important part to play in your church. Sweet people teach you to love by example. Salty people teach you to love by experience. You have to watch your words around salty types. You have to be at your best or you'll get stung. Sweet people are easy to be with. Salty people stretch your character when you're with them. Both have their place, but rough-edged people are the ones who help round off your rough edges.

What to Do with Rough-Edged Church Members

Good family members don't stay away from the Thanksgiving gathering because Aunt Mabel will be there. Neither do they stay away from church because she'll be in attendance. Good families and good churches adapt and compensate for their rough-edged members.

The next time you get the chance to watch a healthy family in action, notice how they handle the difficult member of their tribe. If he or she is hard to be around for long, healthy family members take turns. One will sit next to Aunt Mabel during dinner; another will volunteer to switch seats for dessert. Several people take a shift enduring (and hopefully helping refine) difficult aunts and uncles.

The apostle Paul's first letter to the Corinthians was one of his most transparent letters. In it, Paul describes his personal trials and temptations. Then he turns the attention on his audience. He says,

> You yourselves cheat and do wrong, and you do this
> to your brothers and sisters. Or do you not know that
> wrongdoers will not inherit the kingdom of God?
> Do not be deceived: Neither the sexually immoral
> nor idolaters nor adulterers nor men who have sex
> with men nor thieves nor the greedy nor drunkards
> nor slanderers nor swindlers will inherit the king-
> dom of God. And that is what some of you were.
> But you were washed, you were sanctified, you were
> justified in the name of the Lord Jesus Christ and by
> the Spirit of our God. (1 Corinthians 6:8–11)

Look at that passage again. Specifically, look at the second-to-last sentence: "And that is what some of you were." That little sentence is one of my favorite sentences in the entire Bible because it means there is hope for me, and hope for every person I care about. Look at the list of no-nos for a minute. It includes the sexually immoral, idolaters, adulterers, thieves, greedy people, drunkards, slanderers, and swindlers. It's quite a list, isn't it? That's what the church is supposed to be made up of. "That is what some of you were."

The reason churches aren't perfect is the very reason God loves them so much: churches are made up of sinners like me and you.

The reason churches aren't perfect is the very reason God loves them so much: churches are made up of sinners like me and you.

If you want to get the most out of church, you're going to have to admit that some of the people there will rub you the wrong way and refine you in ways you'd rather not be refined. One of my favorite people was my Auntie Anne. She was one of the kindest, gentlest, most others-centered souls I've ever known. Your church will have some Auntie Annes. You can't help but love them. Others will be Aunt Mabels. You'll have to choose to love them.

Here's the thing, though. If you were to peel back the skin of every prickly churchgoer, underneath you'd find someone worth loving. And if you'll be patient enough to let the Holy Spirit do His work of refining, someday you'll know that once-prickly person as God's miracle of grace. I know several miracles of grace.

Out of the Muck and Mire

Graham Foster is one of the kindest people I know. He's got the wrinkled face of a long-term smoker and the gentle soul of a saint. If you knew him several years ago, you probably wouldn't recognize him today.

Graham's theme verse is Psalm 40:2:

> He lifted me out of the slimy pit,
>
> > out of the mud and mire;
>
> he set my feet on a rock
>
> > and gave me a firm place to stand.

More than twenty years ago, when I was searching for a name for our church, I picked "New Song" because of the verse that follows:

> He put a new song in my mouth,
>
> > a hymn of praise to our God.
>
> Many will see and fear the LORD
>
> > and put their trust in him. (Psalm 40:3)

In a very real way, Graham's story is the story of my church.

Graham grew up in South Africa. His mom died when he was nine. By Graham's description, his dad was not a godly man at all. Graham moved out at age thirteen. He made his way to London, where he got caught up in drugs and alcohol. The majority of his adult life was spent in addiction.

Graham started attending New Song five years ago. His sister and brother-in-law invited him to make the two-hour trek from Los Angeles each weekend. At the time, Graham was homeless. He was living on the streets and, in his own words, "slinging dope and dealing drugs." He says, "I lived that way for ten years. I have no idea how many lives I destroyed by my lifestyle." Fortunately, God has allowed him to help repair a few of them since then.

In church one Easter Sunday, I was explaining the grace of God and the forgiveness available from Jesus when heaven and earth began a wrestling match over Graham's heart and eternity. He told me, "While you were explaining how to have a relationship with Jesus, I was having the struggle of my life. I don't remember it all, but afterward my stepmom told me I was sweating and in tears until the moment I gave in." Jesus was reclaiming Graham, and Satan didn't like it.

Graham says, "God was telling me, 'How much longer do I need to carry you, My son?' While Satan was saying, 'You don't need this. You can make it on your own.' Finally, Jesus took one mighty pull. He lifted me out of my chair and up to the front of the church where I invited Jesus to have my life. He pulled me out of the muck and mire and rescued me from my sin."

You might not have liked Graham before that moment. You certainly wouldn't have approved of his lifestyle. But if you met him today, I think you'd agree with me that he is one of the most enjoyable people you've ever met.

What you can't possibly know until you've seen it is that God is in the reclamation and transformation business. When a person enters into a relationship with Jesus, God's Holy Spirit moves inside that person's soul and begins working on them from the inside out. At the same time, as they enter into the life of the church, God uses sermons, worship experiences, prayers, and the friendship and counsel of others to work from the outside in.

> *God is in the reclamation*
> *and transformation business.*

In every good church, there are those who have been reclaimed and are being transformed, along with those in the queue. Someday the Aunt Mabels you want to throttle will become the Auntie Annes you want to hug.

Here's the key to loving your church. It's my sixth suggestion for making Sunday the best day of your week: *Accept that there are rough-edged people at church, and anticipate that God will round them out.*

Accept that there are rough-edged people at church, and anticipate that God will round them out.

My friend Graham has a tough background. These days, he cries every time he tells his story. "You never get used to His grace. I don't deserve it," he says. "I don't cry because I'm sad. I cry because I am so grateful for what God has done for me."

That's the church. No perfect people need apply. Only those eligible for reclamation and transformation. We're more of a hospital than a museum.

Chapter 7

This One Thing You Must Do

Anyone searching for a new job knows that it's helpful to get some background information on a company before you apply for a position there. Why was the company started? What's its purpose? Who's in charge? And where are they taking it?

For six chapters now we've talked about how church works. In this chapter, I want to show you how churches came to be and why they exist at all. When you understand what I'm about to tell you, you'll see why there is one crucial thing you must do in order to get the most out of your church experience.

To understand church, it helps to know a few things about the Bible and human history.

When you read the Bible from cover to cover, you find one

theme, one thread that winds its way from the first chapter of Genesis to the last chapter of Revelation. The theme is *God's family*.

The story starts with the creation of the world. After crafting the sun and the moon and the stars in the sky, God constructs a perfect place on an orb called earth and populates it with animals, plants, and wonder. In the midst of this paradise He places a man and a woman, self-aware beings who bear His image and likeness. Genesis 3:8 indicates that God's relationship with this couple was so intimate that He took walks with them in the evenings. It was a perfect place with a perfect God in perfect harmony with His creation.

You've heard the story. This man and woman, who had freedom to choose anything they wanted, chose the one thing God asked them to avoid. They ate from the tree God labeled "the tree of the knowledge of good and evil" (Genesis 2:17). It was an act of disobedience, and it fractured their perfect relationship with God.

From that moment until this, God has been about the business of re-creating the original unity He had with His creation. Open a Bible to any page or chapter and you'll find a God who is building a family of people who relate to Him by faith, and He goes to great lengths to do so.

In the second book of the Bible, God introduces a character named Moses. Moses is the great liberator and lawgiver. Backed by ten divinely generated visual aids, Moses liberates the children of Israel from slavery in Egypt. In the Sinai desert he delivers to them God's great law. We call this law the Ten Commandments.

For the next thousand-plus years, the Israelites live under this law. One thing is obvious: though the law is simple, no one can live up to it. Everyone falls short. During this era, God sends prophets to remind the people of His love and to let them know that one day the law will be written on their hearts. Each of the prophets mentions or hints at a coming Deliverer who will make this all possible.

The Christmas Story

At just the right time, the Deliverer comes. He's more of everything good than anyone could have imagined. He's the Son of God, which makes Him perfect and powerful. He's also the son of a woman, which makes Him fully human and able to identify with us in every struggle and temptation. This God-Man, Jesus, proves His divinity by teaching with unparalleled wisdom, healing blind, deaf, and lame people, walking on water, and feeding thousands from mere table scraps. After training twelve men to continue His mission to the world, Jesus announces that He is going to "build my church" (Matthew 16:18). He is so confident of this that He promises not even the gates of hell will prevail against it.

The Easter Story

Jesus then predicts His death. It's a death that emulates the lamb sacrifices Israel has been making for more than a millennium. On

Good Friday morning, Jesus is led like a lamb to the slaughter, up a hill outside of Jerusalem. He dies there, proclaiming, "It is finished" (John 19:30).

It's a curious phrase. What was finished?

Jesus was saying that through His death, God was completing the work He needed to do to rebuild harmony with humans. The fracture that resulted from the disobedience in paradise was being mended. The God who created people was making it possible for people to have a barrier-free relationship with Him again.

How?

By coming to earth and living a perfect, sinless life, Jesus was able to do for us what we could not do for ourselves. Before Adam and Eve ate that first fruit, God had decreed that "when you eat from [the tree of the knowledge of good and evil] you will certainly die" (Genesis 2:17). Adam and Eve ate, and death entered the world. People, plants, and animals have been experiencing death ever since. Not only physical death, humans have been experiencing *spiritual death* because we turned our backs on God.

When Jesus died like a lamb on a hillside, His life paid for our death. It's called "substitution." Like one basketball player entering a game to replace another, Jesus entered into death as our substitute. His death made possible our life. This is the climax of the Bible's story: Jesus's death makes it possible for anyone to become part of God's family. Jesus's sacrifice gives us access to God once again, forever.

The Importance of the Church

This is why the Church is so important. It is God's forever family. It's the community in which He gathers His children. All those who have chosen to let Jesus's death become a substitution for their own death get to enter into what He called "full life" (John 10:10), which means being in relationship with the Lord both here on earth and in the life to come.

A few years ago a lady named Christy asked me, "Can I join the church without becoming a Christian?"

It was a sincere question. What Christy didn't understand was that the Church, God's true Church, is made up *only* of Christians. Let me explain.

When Jesus said, "I will build my church, and the gates of Hades will not overcome it" (Matthew 16:18), the word He used for "church" was the Greek word *ekklesia*. *Ekklesia* means "those who are called out." By definition, Jesus's Church is made up of those who have been called out of separation from God into a relationship with Him through what Jesus did on their behalf. In other words, the Church is made up of those who have chosen to follow Jesus. We call Jesus's followers "Christians." Only Christians can be members of the Church because only Christians *are* members of the Church. In order to become a member of the Church, the one thing you must do is *become a member of God's family*. You do this by accepting what Jesus did for you.

Become a member of God's family.

This has been God's plan for you from the beginning.

Believe and Receive

I explained this to Christy. Then I showed her John 1:12, which says, "To all who did receive [Jesus], to those who believed in his name, he gave the right to become children of God." Can you see the family connection there? The two things we must do to become "children of God" (that is, part of His family) are *believe* and *receive*.

"Believing in Jesus" means believing that He was and is the Son of God who came to earth and died for your shortcomings. "Receiving Jesus" means inviting Him into your life to live in and through you as your Lord and Savior.

A New Creation

Edwin Samson is one of my favorite people. Edwin was a navy hospital corpsman (read "medic") who served two deployments during Operation Iraqi Freedom and helped mend as well as bury several of his comrades-in-arms.

Edwin had gone to church as a youngster, but coming home from war, he vowed never to return again unless God Himself told him to. Edwin used those exact words with his wife one day. The next day, he received a postcard in the mail from my church. He took it as a sign and showed up the following Sunday.

After hearing the story of Jesus, Edwin believed in and received Christ. His life was changed. Edwin started sitting in the front row. Over the next few weeks he began filling the row with friends from work. The Bible says, "If anyone is in Christ, the new creation has come: The old has gone, the new is here!" (2 Corinthians 5:17). Edwin had become a new creation.

It's tempting to hope that once you've received salvation, your life will be one big "happily ever after." But becoming a Christian doesn't guarantee smooth sailing. Jesus's promise is for "full" and eternal life. Edwin's wife left him soon after he became a Christian. Edwin found comfort in Jesus and in members of the church. He returned to college, completed his bachelor's degree, then enrolled in graduate school and completed a master's degree in theology. During this time, God brought a young woman named Amy into his life.

Edwin's experience of being part of the church was so powerful that he told God he would plant a new church for Him somewhere. Today, Edwin and Amy have two wonderful children and are planting a church on an island in the Philippines. Using scuba lessons, computer programming courses, and community development projects, the Samsons are continuing God's story of building His family, one life and one church at a time.

Your Story

Making the most of your church experience starts with becoming a Christian. All you need to do is believe and receive. As a child, I *believed* that Jesus was the second person of the Trinity, that He died on Good Friday for my sins and rose on Easter to conquer death. What I didn't understand is that His salvation is a free gift that has to be *received*. He was offering it, but I had to take it. So like Jill and Graham and Edwin, I reached out my hand to receive Jesus's gift of salvation for me.

You can receive Christ right now by praying a prayer similar to the one Edwin prayed that changed his life. The prayer goes, *"Lord Jesus, I admit I'm a sinner in need of a Savior and I invite You to be mine today. I accept what Jesus did for me on the cross as a substitute for my sin. Come into my life. Live Your life through me, and I will live for You for the rest of my life."*

Most people find it helpful to pray those words out loud. I encourage you to do so now.

A Cosmic Party

As Jesus was getting ready to launch His Church, He told His disciples, "There is rejoicing in the presence of the angels of God over one sinner who repents" (Luke 15:10). If you just prayed that prayer, there is a party going on in heaven right now. Your name is on the banner over the door!

Giving your life to Jesus is the first step in your walk with His family. I guarantee, with Jesus in your life, you will begin to love Sunday, and it will become the most important day of your week. Welcome to the adventure! Practice the seven steps I've outlined in these pages and you will become a deeply joyful and greatly dangerous member of God's family.

Step 1: *Decide to let Sunday be the best day of your week.*

Step 2: *Invest something great into church.*

Step 3: *Honor God's rhythm by celebrating the Sabbath.*

Step 4: *Prepare for Sunday as if it's the highlight of your week.*

Step 5: *Start your children off on the way they should go.*

Step 6: *Accept that there are rough-edged people at church, and anticipate that God will round them out.*

Step 7 (which is really step 1): *Become a member of God's family.*

Three days after Jesus's death on the cross, He rose from the grave on Easter Sunday. That's how the Church got started and why Sunday is such a special day for all Christ followers. The Church is the gathering of the members of Jesus's family. Its effect on history has been stunning.

Conclusion

What the World Would Be Like Without the Church

Once you've become a Christian, you automatically become part of Jesus's family, the Church. Christians *are* the Church. That's one of the reasons it's so important that we become involved in church.

Because the Church is Jesus's family, it does the work of God here on the earth. If you had been there at its very beginning, you could not possibly have predicted the amount of good the Church would do for our world over the next two thousand years.

In AD 33 Jesus Christ forecasted that His message would be preached to every nation in the world (Matthew 24:14). He boldly announced to twelve young men that the gates of hell would not prevail against the organization He was going to build (Matthew 16:18). Both statements could qualify as delusions of grandeur. After all, He was going to die in just a few weeks and He knew it (Matthew 16:21). The place He was living was a backwater nation governed by a foreign power. The people He was talking to were uneducated teenagers. How could a dozen adolescents with a dead leader create the most widespread movement in history?

Fast-forward two thousand years and Jesus's Church is the largest organization on earth. More than two billion churchgoers gather every weekend in every country on the planet. From cathedrals to classrooms, in apartments and assembly halls, under trees and in caves, Christians meet for church anywhere and everywhere. Just as Jesus said they would.

How did this happen?

Follow Me

Skim through the Gospel records and you'll find thirteen times when Jesus makes a two-word request of His disciples: "Follow me." It's His most frequently repeated phrase. By it, Jesus was asking His followers to imitate His values and actions. "Follow me" means "Do as I do. Think as I think. Love people the way I love them."

The disciples took His request seriously. Wherever they went, they cared for people, listening to their hurts, healing them when possible, proclaiming the good news that God was real and had come to earth in the form of a man named Jesus.

Those original disciples followed Jesus to Greece, Turkey, Spain, Italy, India, Africa, and parts in between. Within a century, Christianity had spread throughout the Mediterranean Basin. Wherever they went, they loved people so authentically that their faith was contagious.

New religions were illegal in the Roman Empire, so Christians were persecuted. Sometimes their belongings were seized. Other times their bodies were burned or fed to lions or used as gladiator-fodder in the Roman Circus Colosseum. Instead of scaring people *from* Christianity, these heroic acts drew people *to* the Church. No one could argue about the sincerity of Christians' beliefs. So the movement grew.

In AD 313, Constantine issued the Edict of Milan, which legalized Christianity. Christians began to build churches. At the Council of Nyssa, a gathering of church leaders, it was decided that whenever a cathedral was built, the church would also build a hospital next door.

In an attempt to follow Jesus, Christians invented the idea of a charitable organization. Study the roots of the Red Cross, the YMCA, the Salvation Army, World Vision, Compassion International, or Samaritan's Purse, and you'll discover they were all founded by Christians.

A few years ago I was invited to speak at a church in Nairobi, Kenya. (If you're tempted to be impressed, don't be. The pastor, Francis Kamau, is a friend of mine. I was in the country on other business, and he was polite enough to invite me to speak.) When the service was over, one of the church members drove me back to my hotel. As we left the church parking lot, we turned onto a large boulevard. The driver said, "See this boulevard? Two years ago, when we decided to build our church here, this street was full of bars and brothels. Now look at it." I looked and saw nicely dressed businessmen, normal families, and a general aura of peace. "Most of the bars are closed now, and many of the former prostitutes are now members of our church."

This scenario has been repeated thousands of times in hundreds of cities over the last two thousand years. I love Sundays because Sundays are church days, and church days change lives.

I love Sundays because Sundays are church days, and church days change lives.

Why I Love the Church

Wherever you find the Church, you'll find flaws and failures because the Church is made up of people. We're all flawed failures who recognize that we need Jesus's help to have any hope for full life here and in the age to come. It's easy to love Jesus; He's perfect. It's not easy to love the Church. But the truth is, the Church has done more good for the world than any other institution in history.

A few years after I rejoined the church, I was sitting in my youth pastor's office when he said something I'll never forget. He said, "I love the church." To this day I remember how ridiculous that statement sounded to me. Where I grew up, the church was an old stone building filled with ancient smells and religious symbols. *How could anyone love the church?*

For forty years now, I've been part of a local church. I've witnessed heartaches, disappointments, disagreements, embarrassments, and shame. But I have also participated in moments of joy, hope, peace, and love. I've seen help offered, hugs given, addictions overcome, lives turned around, relationships mended, and eternities changed. The Church is the most exciting organization on earth.

Jesus came for the Church, died for the Church, and returned to heaven where He intercedes at the right hand of His Father for the Church. The leadership of Jesus and the power of the Holy Spirit reside in the Church. That's why the Church is the hope of the world.

Jesus came for the Church, died for the Church, and returned to heaven where He intercedes at the right hand of His Father for the Church.

The Church isn't a building. It's a body, a family, a flock, and an army.[1] It's the living, breathing life of Jesus here on earth today.

The Bride

In the final book of the Bible, just before the re-creation of the new heaven and the new earth, God describes for us what He intended for His people all along. Revelation 19:7 depicts a wedding, called "The wedding of the Lamb." Jesus is the Lamb, and His Church is the bride. We are united to Him in a ceremony that makes a rock concert look tame and a Super Bowl victory seem boring. An angel declares, "Blessed are those who are invited to the wedding supper of the Lamb!" (Revelation 19:9).

The writer of Revelation then describes this incredible feast at the climax of history. It's a passage well worth reading and a moment well worth waiting for. In fact, I've staked my life on that moment. See, the Bible says that at the end of time there will be a great celebration where Jesus will be united with His people, and the only thing that will matter in that moment is what you did to help Him build the thing that matters most to Him—His Church.

That's the day that matters. That's the day when Jesus will look you in the eyes and tell you what He thought of your life. If you start to bring up your sins, He'll say, "Do you remember the day you asked Me to forgive you? That's the day I stopped remembering all of that."

Well Done

In Matthew 25, Jesus tells a story that has become known as "The Parable of the Talents." A "talent" was a huge sum of gold. According to Jesus's story, each of the master's servants is given a bag or more of gold to invest in the building of the master's business. At the end of the story, the master doesn't ask his servants about the mistakes they've made. He only asks about their bags of gold. Those who have multiplied what he gave them hear a loud, "Well done, good and faithful servant!" The one who missed the point of the investment and did nothing with it hears, "You wicked, lazy servant!"

More than anything in this life, I want to hear "well done" in the next life. I'm living every day for that day. Because at the end of time, I won't care where I lived, what car I drove, or what titles I earned. The only thing that will matter is the approval of Jesus. And it's all measured by the investment of my life in the enhancement of His Church. I love the church, and I love Sundays because Sundays at church lay the foundation for so much of the good that goes on during the rest of the week. In fact, not only do I want to make Sunday the best day of my week, my goal is to make Sunday the best day of the week for every person possible. I invite you to join me in this work.

Notes

Chapter 1: Why I Came Back to Church

1   "That's What I Love About Sunday," music and lyrics by Mark Narmore, Adam Dorsey. Copyright: Ole Media Management O.B.O. Cake Taker Music, Ole Media Management O.B.O. Drivers Ed. Music.

2   James C. Patterson II, MD, PhD, "Live Long and Prosper: Going to Church Increases Lifespan," Reasons to Believe, August 20, 2010, http://www.reasons.org/articles/live-long-and-prosper-going-to-church-increases-lifespan.

3   Janet Washington, "New Study: Regular Church Attendance Linked to Positive Outlook, Less Depression in Women," *EEEW Magazine Buzz*, November 11, 2011, http://buzz.eewmagazine.com/eew-magazine-buzz-blog/2011/11/11/new-study-regular-church-attendance-linked-to-positive-outlo.html.

4   Washington.

5   W. Bradford Wilcox, quoted in Glenn T. Stanton, "First-Person: The Christian Divorce Rate Myth (What You've Heard Is Wrong)," *Baptist Press*, February 15, 2011, http://www.bpnews.net/34656#top.

6   Scott M. Stanley et al., "Marriage in Oklahoma: 2001 Baseline Statewide Survey on Marriage and Divorce," http://www.okmarriage.org/downloads/media/survey_report.pdf.

7   Peter Haas, "The Jaw Dropping Benefits of Church Attendance," *PeterHaas*, August 19, 2014, http://www.peter-haas.org/?p=1342.

Chapter 2: What Church Was Meant to Be

1   True confession: I'm a pastor. In fact, I'm not just a pastor, I'm a church planter. I actually planted the church I now lead. Coming back to church was such a good decision for me that I decided to start a church for other people. As our church has gotten bigger, I've had to turn over the responsibility for calling first-time guests to a team of volunteers who do a better job at it than I am able to do.

2   PromiseLand is our children's Sunday school program.

Chapter 3: What You Really Want out of Church

1   Hal Seed, *The Bible Questions: Shedding Light on the World's Most Important Book* (Downers Grove, IL: IVP Books, 2012).

Chapter 4: How to Make Sunday the High Point of Your Week

1   "Shabbat," *Jewish.tv*, http://www.chabad.org/multimedia/media_cdo/aid/141138/jewish/Shabbat.htm.

Chapter 5: How to Make Sunday the High Point of Your Children's Week

1   Jesus's exact words in Matthew 6:33 are "Seek first his kingdom and his righteousness, and all these things will be given to you as well."

2   Jesus's exact words in Luke 6:40 are "Everyone who is fully trained will be like their teacher."

Conclusion: What the World Would Be Like Without the Church

1   Colossians 1:24; Ephesians 2:20; 1 Peter 5:2; 2 Timothy 2:3.

About the Author

As pastor of the largest church immediately south of Marine Corps Base Camp Pendleton, Dr. Hal Seed has been called "America's Pastor to the Marine Corps." Hal and his wife, Lori, founded New Song Community Church in Oceanside, California, in 1992. New Song is a multiethnic, multicampus church ministering to all ages, stages, and social strata. At this writing, New Song has seen more than 17,000 people decide to follow Jesus. Hal believes so strongly in the power of church that he and New Song have helped impact the planting of more than 200,000 churches worldwide. Hal and Lori have two grown children and a growing number of grand-children. He mentors pastors at www.pastormentor.com.

Hal is the author of five books, including *The God Questions*, published by Outreach, Inc. Together, *The God Questions* and *The God Questions, Gift Edition* have sold more than 300,000 copies, helping many people know God better.